THE SENSES

The Sense of Smell

by Mari Schuh

Consultant:
Eric H. Chudler, Ph.D.
Director, Neuroscience for Kids
University of Washington
Seattle, Wash.

BLASTOFF! 4 READERS

BELLWETHER MEDIA • MINNEAPOLIS, MN

Note to Librarians, Teachers, and Parents:

Blastoff! Readers are carefully developed by literacy experts and combine standards-based content with developmentally-appropriate text.

Level 1 provides the most support through repetition of high-frequency words, light text, predictable sentence patterns, and strong visual support.

Level 2 offers early readers a bit more challenge through varied simple sentences, increased text load, and less repetition of high frequency words.

Level 3 advances early-fluent readers toward fluency through increased text and concept load, less reliance on visuals, longer sentences, and more literary language.

Level 4 builds reading stamina by providing more text per page, increased use of punctuation, greater variation in sentence patterns, and increasingly challenging vocabulary.

Level 5 encourages children to move from "learning to read" to "reading to learn" by providing even more text, varied writing styles, and less familiar topics.

Whichever book is right for your reader, Blastoff! Readers are the perfect books to build confidence and encourage a love of reading that will last a lifetime!

This edition first published in 2008 by Bellwether Media.

No part of this publication may be reproduced in whole or in part without written permission of the publisher. For information regarding permission, write to Bellwether Media Inc., Attention: Permissions Department, Post Office Box 1C, Minnetonka, MN 55345-9998.

Library of Congress Cataloging-in-Publication Data
Schuh, Mari C., 1975–
  The sense of smell / by Mari Schuh.
    p. cm. — (Blastoff! readers. The senses)
Summary: "Introductory text explains the function and experience of the sense of smell. Intended for grades two through five"—Provided by publisher.
  Includes bibliographical references and index.
  ISBN-13: 978-1-60014-072-3 (hardcover : alk. paper)
  ISBN-10: 1-60014-072-6 (hardcover : alk. paper)
  1. Smell–Juvenile literature. I. Title.

  QP458.S38 2008
  612.8'6–dc22   2007018841

Contents

Your Sense of Smell

Breathe in through your nose and sniff. What do you smell?

Maybe you smell your dirty clothes or food cooking in the kitchen. You're using your sense of smell.

Smelling is only one of your senses. Your other senses are sight, hearing, touch, and taste. Your nose and your brain work together to smell. So how do you smell different **scents**?

fun fact

People can smell about 3,000 to 10,000 scents That's a lot of different smells!

How Smelling Works

It starts with tiny **particles** you can't see. For example, particles from a pot of soup float in the air.

When you breathe in, the particles move into your nose. They stick to **mucus** inside your nose.

9

Your nose has **sensors**. Sensors send a message about the particles. The message travels to the brain along thin threads of tissue called **nerves**. Your brain gets the message. Then your brain tells you about the smell.

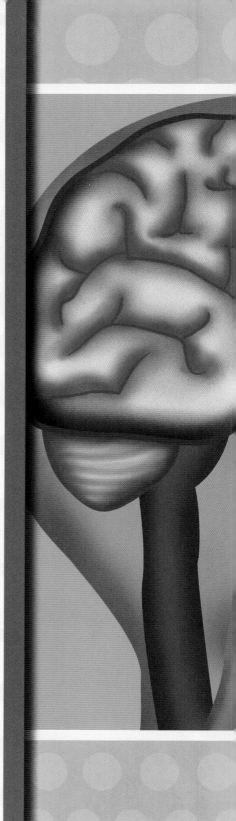

fun fact

Your sense of smell isn't very good in the morning. You can smell things better later in the day.

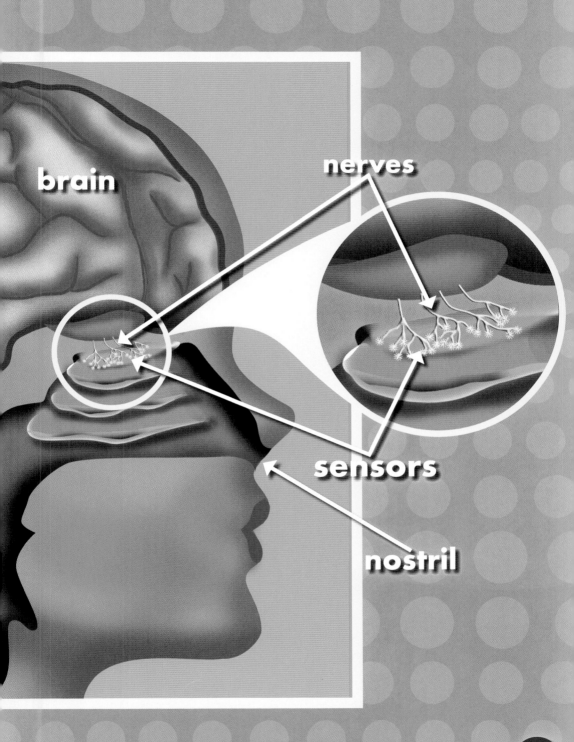

brain

nerves

sensors

nostril

Your brain can tell you about thousands of scents. Maybe the scent of freshly cut grass smells good to you. Onions and coffee might smell bad to you.

Some scents can bring back memories. Perfume or flowers might remind you of your grandma. Turkey might make you think of Thanksgiving.

Smelling and Tasting

Your sense of smell even helps you taste food! You breathe in and smell food as you eat.

Try it! Eat a piece of food. Then pinch your nose and take another bite. The taste of the second bite won't be nearly as strong.

fun fact

Some people can't smell at all. About 2 million people in the United States have no sense of smell. This problem is called anosmia.

Food also tastes dull when you
have a cold. Thick mucus stuffs
up your nose.

The mucus makes it hard for particles to get to the sensors in your nose.

17

Animals and Smell

Many animals have a better sense of smell than people. Dogs have millions more smell sensors than people.

Dogs use their noses to sniff out food and other dogs. Some dogs use their sense of smell to help find missing people.

Smelling Danger

Smelling is important. It can help you sense danger. The smell of rotten food keeps you from eating it. You know a fire is nearby when you smell smoke.

Your sense of smell tells you about your surroundings. Sniff around. What scents do you smell?

fun fact
Our sense of smell gets worse as we get older.

Glossary

mucus—a slippery substance that protects the inside of your mouth, nose, and throat; mucus also catches food particles.

nerves—thin strings of tissue throughout your body; nerves carry messages between your brain and other parts of your body.

particle—a tiny piece of something

scent—the smell of something

sensor—the parts of your body that send messages to your nerves and brain

To Learn More

AT THE LIBRARY
Barraclough, Sue. *What Can I Smell?* Chicago, Ill.: Raintree, 2005.

Mackill, Mary. *Smelling*. Chicago, Ill.: Heinemann, 2006.

Rau, Dana Meachen. *Sniff, Sniff: A Book about Smell*. Minneapolis, Minn.: Picture Window Books, 2005.

ON THE WEB
Learning more about smell
is as easy as 1, 2, 3.

1. Go to www.factsurfer.com

2. Enter "smell" into search box.

3. Click the "Surf" button and you will see a list of related web sites.

With factsurfer.com, finding more information is just a click away.

Index

The images in this book are reproduced through the courtesy of: Grafissimo, front cover; North Georgia Media, p. 4; White Packert/Getty Images, p. 5; Johner/Getty Images, pp. 6- 7; marmion, p. 8; Veer Steve Cicero/Getty Images, p. 9; Linda Clavel, pp. 10-11; Mike Powell/Getty Images, p. 12; Julie DeGuia, p. 13; David P. Hall/Masterfile, pp. 14-15; Steven May, p. 16; Bronwyn Photo, p. 17; Jostein Hauge, p. 18; Alberto Biscar/Masterfile, p. 19; Kevin Summers/Getty Images, p. 20; Ethan Meleg/ Getty Images, p. 21.